BEYOND MILLIONAIRE'S THINKING

CHANGE THAT BRINGS

ABOUT

GREAT WEALTH

Abimbola Cole Idris

TESTIMONIES:

These are testimonies from readers of other books written by the same author.

1. Abimbola Cole Idris you are truly a genius in your area of expertise, I respect you greatly. I read your book titled "How To Become A Millionaire in A Way That Is Dignifying To God" and my life has never been the same since then.

   Jonathan Williams from USA

2. Abimbola Cole Idris your book titled "How To Conquer The Spirit Of Fear And Become A Millionaire" is a winner, it conveys a wealth of information and it is value for money.

   Stephen from United Kingdom

3. Truly superb. Abimbola Cole Idris delivers the principles of being a millionaire in an innovative and provoking way that is bound to change anybody else's life also. I am truly grateful for having read this book. Abimbola Cole's Book is unquestionably up there with the likes of Rich Dad Poor Dad.

   Daniel Billios from Greece

4. The outstanding breath-taking book titled "How To Become A Millionaire In A Way That Is Dignifying To God" this book is truly a winner and also the best book I have read in years. It is truly an inspiring and motivating book. Many thanks to this intelligent author, Abimbola Cole Idris.

   Tunde Adedayo from Nigeria

BEYOND MILLIONAIRE'S THINKING

CHANGE THAT BRINGS ABOUT GREAT WEALTH

BY

ABIMBOLA COLE IDRIS

iUniverse, Inc.
New York   Bloomington

BEYOND MILLIONAIRE'S THINKING
CHANGE THAT BRINGS ABOUT GREAT WEALTH

iUniverse books may be ordered through booksellers or by contacting:

iUniverse
1663 Liberty Drive
Bloomington, IN 47403
www.iuniverse.com
1-800-Authors (1-800-288-4677)

Because of the dynamic nature of the Internet, any Web addresses or links contained in this book may have changed since publication and may no longer be valid. The views expressed in this work are solely those of the author and do not necessarily reflect the views of the publisher, and the publisher hereby disclaims any responsibility for them.

ISBN: 978-1-4401-2477-8 (pbk)
ISBN: 978-1-4401-2476-1 (ebk)

Library of Congress Control Number: 2009925382

Printed in the United States of America

iUniverse rev. date: 3/27/09

Reference: The following people have inspired me and I found their advices very useful.

Mark Victor Hansen, Robert Kiyosaki, Robert Allen, and Mike Litman, these people are great leaders and genius of our times.

Book I found useful: The principles of psychology by James W (1890) Henry Holt New York.

ABSTRACT

This book aims to teach the reader and lead him or her, by hands, through the journey of becoming a millionaire and very successful.

It is a true story. It is a principle which the author herself, and many others have put into practice and which has helped them become successful.

Therefore it can work for you as well, but the trick is that you must take actions by putting into practice what is written in the book. The principles need to be applied first then you will get the results

I can see you fulfilling your dreams, bringing your dreams into reality, and becoming a millionaire very soon. Even sooner than you ever thought possible, so shall it be (Amen).

ACKNOWLEDGEMENT

This book is dedicated to my late father Mr T A Lawal and all motherless babies around the world.

And to all present and future millionaires to be and also to who ever comes in contact with this book.

CONTENTS

INTRODUCTION

This is a book written after ten years of research to find out why some people are poor and some are stinking rich.

In this book you will discover how it happens. The book will reveal to you the steps you need to take and your life will never be the same again. It will provide you with the inspiration and mindset of a successful person. I want you to know, without a doubt in your mind, that it is possible for you to become a successful and rich person regardless of your financial or education background. You deserve a life of happiness and abundance, once you make up your mind, you are unstoppable and there are no limitations based on your religion, gender or race. You can become a successful entrepreneur starting new businesses. Now is your time, this moment is better than ever for you to become financially successful.

You will discover five important concepts of progressing in life, Six steps to make your dreams a reality, Five ideas on what to do in order to progress, Five laws that will help you keep your customer, and finally, Four important ways to keep your business expanding and three secrets you need for real estate to work for you.

CHAPTER ONE

FIVE CONCEPTS OF PROGRESS

Concept 1: You Need a Good Mind Set

What is mind set?

Mind set is a mental reaction that determines how a person will interpret or react to any thing and everything or even a circumstance at any particular time. The mind is a very powerful possession of value that we as human-being possess. If you use it correctly, it will work in a good way for you. The mind is everything to human beings. If you set it right, you can have and enjoy every good thing on earth. In other words you can enjoy your heaven on earth if your mind set is properly handled.

Anything you set your mind on to achieve is possible, including setting your mind to become a dignified millionaire. Please, I will advice you not to ever underestimate the power of the mind. The mind is a precious property which every human being must cherish and protect. I am protecting mine and so should you.

Do you know that many people have not achieved their prospect in life because of their mind set? Even though they have what it takes to achieve everything they want in life but they are not there yet due to their mind set. Make up your mind today. Have a millionaire's thinking mind, set up your mind and become a self made millionaire very soon. You can develop a unique mindset for success. You can move at a super speed to become a successful and self made millionaire.

You need a millionaire's mindset. This is a key component to success and wealth creation. Whatever your financial background or situations are, if you start to think and act like a millionaire, you will soon become one. You need to change from limiting mindset to abundant thinking mindset. Do you know that when you think in abundant you will create a wealth life and happy lifestyle, while thoughts of lack would create a life of scarcity, shortage and insufficient?

There are two types of mind set:

- A Positive, unstoppable mind set
- A Negative, downward mind set

A positive mind set is when you set your mind in a way that it delivers positive things to you, such as using your mind set to achieve any good thing you set your mind at to achieve. However, On the other hand, a negative mind set will only deliver negative things and setback to its owner. In other words when your mind set is negative you will continually think of negative things. And believe it or not what ever you think of regularly and constantly over a period of time you will achieve whether one likes it or not.

The story of Meredith (written with consent)

Meredith is divorced and a mother of five children. Her ordeal started when her husband left her for a younger woman four years ago. She revealed that the last four years of her life has being that of emotional torture, pain and anguish, she said many a night, both she and the kids went to bed with empty bellies. She recalled a night when the little girl who is five years old had to cry all through the night as she was hungry and couldn't sleep.

Meredith said the moment her husband left her, She felt that the whole world has collapsed on her, she became hopeless with all her hope, good will and positive attitude went down the drain as nothing appeals or makes sense to her any more. She began to think in a box, she constantly think about lack, scarcity and insufficiency, until she met the author of this book, who worked continuously with her for three months on how to renew her mind, think positive and achieve whatever she wants on earth. She was told that each thought she had was manifested in her mind. She determined to change her thought from lack to many and abundant, and then thing began to change for her.

Meredith is now a very happy woman running her own private and successful businesses and controlling a fat bank account. She is building wealth via entrepreneurship, real estate and stock market investing, publishing, product development, and other avenue of wealth creation. She is following very closely all the advice given to her by the author of this book and most of them you will come across as you read on.

What are your unique talents or strengths? Meredith and others turned theirs into wealth, you can too. You can leverage your creativity skills to wealth and success. I want you to be successful like many of the people I mentored. I therefore challenge you to examine your present thoughts and how they are creating limitations for you, then make all necessary changes and begin to enjoy your way to success and wealth. Most millionaires are just like you and me, they never start as a millionaire, but they become one. It is my wish to give you the same method and secret that was given to those people I mentored which they used and which turned them to self made millionaires.

Hints: You need to constantly dream about the future, dream big dreams, map out plans to take you there, start today, and do not wait until tomorrow as tomorrow may be too late.

FIVE REASONS WHY YOU NEED A GOOD AND POSITIVE MIND SET:

I call it the Bimbolic 5 **I**s formula of success

- It is **Important**
- It is **Inspiring**
- You will be able to **Impinge** in your life.
- It is **Imperative**
- It is **impressive**

IMPORTANT:

A good mind set is important because it is capable of having a great effect on one's life decisions. The mind set should have a greater priority over every other thing in a man's decision making process. Once the mind set is right every other thing are bound to fall in place including money making decisions which is also very important in human life.

For instance, if you have so many things to do, you will automatically put them in order, one thing after the other in order to be able to achieve them systematically. This means they are put in order as a matter of their importance.

Let us use an example to expatiate this further. I will take you on a medical journey because I will like to use my medical background here.

With this scenario below, let's work it out together and make a decision as a matter of importance what part of John's health issue we are going to deal with first in order to treat him and save his life.

Scenario:

John is a 29 year old married man with two beautiful children whom he cares for on his own as his wife is seriously ill and presently in the hospital. She has being in the hospital for the past 3 months. Suddenly John himself developed a weight loosing problem and within two weeks he had already lost 6kg.

Therefore John was advised to come into the hospital. On arrival in the hospital, John was found bleeding continuously, externally not internally from a very big injury on his chest close to his heart. On interrogation John said he got injured on his way to the hospital. If we need to treat John's health issues as a matter of importance, which aspect of his health are we going to look into first?

I am sure every body will agree with me that we need to sort the bleeding aspect out first and then come back to the issue of weight lost otherwise John may bleed to death. You must learn to give your mind setting a priority above other things in order to prevent your ideas and dreams from dying. In the next paragraph let us look into mind setting as inspiring.

INSPIRING:

A good mind set will motivate and give you some sudden business ideas of which, if taken seriously and acted upon, could turn into a money generating machine for you. Take action today on all those things you have been dreaming about, overcome the spirit of procrastination.

IMPINGE:

With a good mind set you will be able to make an impact on your life and even the lives of others around you in a positive way. Once you are able to make a good impact on your life through your mind set and your decision making, then you will be in the position to decide for yourself which route you will like to tread in order to become successful.

Be it to become rich through working hard to achieve your money freedom by following your goals or to just stay floating and rely on others to make your life decisions for you and then pay you what they think you are worth.

Beloved, the decision is yours. Wake up today, and take hold of your life and those of your future generations. Determine to start making decisions that will give you financial freedom soon. I believe in you, you also should believe in yourself and start on your route to making cool and genuine money from today.

Looking back into your life in a few years to come, I want you to be glad that you have taken the decisions to take hold of your own life and pay yourself how much you think you are worth.

IMPERATIVE:

Having your mind set in a positive way is essential and urgently required because every day you delay and do not take those necessary actions you loss money. You need to have a millionaire's mind set that will begin to make millions for you instantly.

Some people may say but I don't need millions in my life to survive. I disagree with that because you do, I know you do. Why not make this money in millions, use what you need from it and then use the remaining to look after the needy.

In life, our mind setting decision is likened to the above scenario where it is seen exactly like the bleeding aspect of John's health issue. We set our mind first and we get our lives right or on the other hand, we leave our mind setting till the last and our dream in life may die.

IMPRESIVE:

Once you are able to make a good and positive mind set, you are on your way to achieving your goals. The moment you begin to achieve them then you will be able to experience that deep feeling of achievement.

What are the benefits of having a positive mindset to my life, in other words how do I benefit from applying a positive mind set to my life?

- Everything about you will look positive and become possible.
- When you apply a positive mindset, your life will be unstoppable; you will continue to be glad all the way through your life.
- Where others around you and, in the same situation with you are crying, lamenting, or even calling a pity party and feeling down, you are using those terrible situations to your own advantage.
- You are busy making money from the messy situations which others think are useless.
- You are seeing the situation with a positive mind.
- You are saying to yourself "although the situation appears ugly, what can I do to turn it to my own advantage?"

- You are thinking how can I make millions out of this circumstance?
- You are busy saying to yourself "how can I make others see the advantages attached to this predicament?"

Do you know that any situation you find yourself in can actually be turned around for your own good and benefit.

In order to experiment this, we compared two people with similar education, training, and personality. Tom and Jerry (of course not their true names). These two men set a goal to be successful and make millions of money, and they migrated to two different countries. After three years, they both came back to the originated country where they migrated from.

Do you know that findings revealed that Tom surpassed his goals easily as he is already enjoying some good money and a lovely life style, simply because he decided to act on his decisions regardless of whatever problem comes his way, while Jerry is still struggling and not able to achieve anything? He went empty handed and came back empty handed.

The difference between these two people's achievement lies on the decisions and actions taken by both men. One made the right decision, stuck to it and was also committed to it, while the other man either never made a decision, or did make one but never got committed to it. Whatever it is, come with me on this adventure and you will find out in a minute as you open up and read on.

I'm sure the next question in your mind is how did this happen? Well relax, make yourself a cup of coffee and I will tell you.

*H*OW DID THIS HAPPEN?

After working with thousands of people to achieve success in their lives, I have found out one common truth: **It is people's Mind Set.** Mind set differentiates between a successful man and the unsuccessful one. It is the difference between the people who are achieving their goals daily and those who are stagnant and not achieving anything good in life.

Do you know that a hundred and one thoughts passes through peoples mind's every day? Do you know that many of them use energy, which can either be positive or negative energy? It is a choice you can choose which ever one you like. Beloved, do you also realise that these types of energy propel us towards taking actions?

The thoughts help us to decide on what action we need to take regarding the situation at hand.

Fredrick's story

Fredrick is one of the cleaners in one of our firms. One morning I had a knock on my office door. "Come in" I said not knowing who was at the other side of the door. Here comes in Fredrick one of the cleaners, "Good morning miss" said Fredrick. Morning Fred how can I help you? I replied. I.., I .., I'm sorry to disturb you miss, but I needed to speak with somebody before I finally give up on myself, and he started crying. I offered Fredrick a chair, gave him a pack of tissue, made him a cup of tea and ask him what the problem was. Miss I am only 25years old, but I constantly feels hopeless and under achieving said Fredrick. I love to become an accountant, and I have all the required subject to become an accountant at A levels but my problem is that whenever It occurs to me to take steps in becoming an accountant, there is always a thought in my head saying "no you can't? How many people in your family is an accountant"? How then do you think you can become one? and I have always believed that voice. Please help me miss, what should I do? My heart desire is to become an accountant.

I advised Fredrick to stop crying and told him that if he allows me to work with him, together we would be able to achieve his heart desire. I asked him to bring in his credentials to me the following morning which he did. Immediately we started applying to universities for accounting courses. Fred was very lucky as he got an admission the same year.

Fredrick successfully completed his accountancy course, graduated as an accountant, went back to his home country and started a massive accounting firm, where he employed other accountants working for him. Fredrick is doing extremely well and his companies are yielding him six figures amount every year. He is a nice young man who is forever grateful, and always sending me letters of appreciations.

I taught Fredrick how to tune the voice of negativity down and to belief strongly in himself and his ability to achieve success. Fredrick had to deal with his doubt and come to belief that anything he wants in life is possible. He was made to belief that all he wanted is already accomplished in his future. He was taught how to create a strong and undoubted dream with clarity, good understanding with one hundred percent energy. These type of dreams need to be strong, challenging, unshakeable and realistic.

Every one I mentored knows the importance of writing a step-by-step plan so that nothing can stop them from achieving what they have set out for.

If Fredrick had continued listening to the negative thoughts and not took the decision to speak to someone and take necessary actions, today he might still be a cleaner.

WHAT THOUGHTS CAN DO IN PEOPLE'S LIVES?

Thoughts are capable of doing mainly two things.

- Firstly, thoughts can create limitation on people's progress over and over again and these can stop people from reaching their goals and achieving their success and moving to a higher level in life.

- Secondly, thoughts can create unstoppable system that can propel people to achieve their goals in no time. It can make people achieve continuous success and overcome progress blocks

Do you know that the latter is the type of thought that most millionaires and successful people use to their advantage in order to achieve their wealth? I constantly taught every one I mentored on how to deal with their thoughts.

In the research with Tom and Jerry, there were so many interviews. During one of these interviews with Jerry, to find out why he was not able to achieve his goals, he revealed that he always felt stuck. He said he knows what he wanted and that he needed to achieve something but he just couldn't achieve them for one reason or the other. He said he knew what was good for him and what he wanted in life, but it was just not happening. He said he remembered that on several occasions he battles with negative thoughts in his mind and he just did not know what to do.

Jerry said that he realized he was trying hard but feeling unfulfilled and unhappy with where he was but just couldn't achieve the breakthrough he needed. Jerry said he found himself rolling in circles, unable to achieve another level. At a point, I asked Jerry whether or not he was able to change the way he thought about things he said no, that his thinking still remain the same.

At this point I asked Jerry if he would allow me to work with him. He answered yes. Then I brought out my dairy and booked an appointment for him to come and see me and then we started working together.

The first approach with Jerry was to teach him how to adjust his mindset, and the second stage was to train him on how to constantly have positive thoughts

Then set a goal of what he wants to achieve and started working on it. Six months later Jerry had already achieved most of what he set on his goal.

IF YOU ALWAYS DO WHAT YOU ALWAYS DO YOU WILL ALWAYS GET WHAT YOU ALWAYS GOT:

Friends, have you ever heard about this saying that "**If you always perform the same activities, you will always get what you always got**". Brother and sister, you need to change the way you have always done things in order to be able to get new results. You should make up your mind to start doing what you have never done in order to get what you have never got. You need to be able to take some risks. Many times there are some breakthroughs behind a risk taken. You need to start breaking into new grounds. Start thinking big and acting big. Think business, eat business, sleep business and wake up with business.

What limitations have you created based on your thought, background and race? Now breathe in deeply and out forcefully, release them and let them go and then realize that wealth knows no boundaries. Many self made millionaires have proven that wealth is not based on race, age or gender. If these people can defy all odds to become successful, you can too.

In order to get to where you want to get to, which is from nowhere to somewhere, from nobody to somebody, I mean from a poor person to a millionaire, you need to develop a good mind set for becoming successful in live and in no time you will become a millionaire". The next question you want to ask me is how then do I set a smart mind set? It's easy, and I will tell you.

HOW TO HAVE A SMART MIND SET:

The main thing is to realize that how we see ourselves, our personality, our career, our jobs, our success and many more **"determines the reality for us"** The way we see a situation determines what result we get from it. If we see a situation in a negative, non-achievable way, our thought about that situation is 'impossible' those thoughts will cause us to act in a way that keeps us from achieving our aims and objectives regarding the issue or situation.

However, if we see a situation as positive, as another opportunity for a breakthrough, as a powerful and a purposeful situation, then we will achieve what we have set out for. Beloved, start working on your thoughts today and you will be amazed at your positive outcomes. Begin to achieve those things that you never thought could be possible for you to achieve.

Therefore to set a goal you need to have something in mind that you want to achieve (a dream that you want to turn into a reality or an idea to turn into a product or service). Once you know what you want, then you need to sit down in a quiet environment and instruct your mind to think, find and derive a plan you need to follow in other to achieve the aim. You need to do these under no pressure, and you need to be well relaxed in a comfortable environment.

Grab your computer and write your ideas down as they are coming to your head. Some of the things that are coming to you might not make sense to you right this moment, but don't worry. Just keep brain storming, keep on writing them down because they will make sense to you later.

Now I assumed you have finished writing it down. If that is the case then rearrange what you have written in a way that one comes after the other making sense to you this time.

After you have successfully done that, commit yourself to a starting date and stick to it come rain or shine, just continue to follow through. We will discuss the best way to follow through in chapter one concept five.

Kate's story

Kate's ambition includes becoming a millionaires, she approached me and asked me to mentor her. I agreed to work with Kate, first I encouraged her to brainstorm. She came up with these lovely ideals, which my team asked her to arrange in steps. After putting her ideas in a step-by-step plan, Kate said she was afraid of failure and did not want to carry out her plans. She said the first step seems the hardest to her. Then Kate was taught how to use her faith. I told her to put her faith into action; she was encouraged to identify a starting date and to start. She was told that once she starts she would gear into motion. And that once she is in motion it will be easier to go from step to step until she gets to the last and final step. She did, and we showed her how to achieve these steps one after the other. Kate is doing very well. She is almost half way through her goals, congratulations Kate.

Since thoughts with negative system or limiting thinking can prevent us from achieving our optimum goals, it will be necessary to identify and erase them off our mind instantly. Brainstorming is an important aspect of goal achieving.

Tamara's story

Tamara is 42years old mother of two who refused to change her old ways of doing things. She believed that she knows it all. Tamara says you can never go wrong doing things the way you have always done it but I made her realized that although she might not go wrong but she will continue to stay on the same level and never achieve another level.

Tamara said there is no point for her to keep trying since she had tried and failed on many occasion. First I made her to realize that she has never failed is just that she hasn't got it right and she should keep trying. During my interview with Tamara, I found out that all she needs to kick start again is courage. I made her to understand that for human being to achieve success obstacles will occur, but the difference between those who succeed and those who do not is how they deal with, or react to these road blocks. I told her a roadblock is only temporary, and it is also an opportunity in disguise.

People learn from most obstacles, and once they overcome it, they would have solution to such obstacles in future and may even be in position to give lectures on such topics. Tamara was encouraged to write out her step-by-step plan and to keep on executing her plans as it takes courage to keep going when it comes to peoples dream. I explained to her that if she keeps going regardless of obstacle, in the end she will enjoy the fruits of her labour when she begins to enjoy the comfort that wealth brings as well as the joy of her achievement. It is my wish that my readers don't only enjoy the joy of wealth only in term of money but also in term of the joy that comes with their success. You need to write a step-by-step plan of your dream, belief in yourself, have the faith to start, have the courage to carry on and have the health to live long to enjoy your wealth.

The next question is 'how then do I identify the limiting thinking and deal with then? It's easy, and this is how.

HOW DO I IDENTIFY THAT WICKED LIMITING THINKING?

Use what I call "The Revealing/ Exposing method or Power whatever you like to call it. This allows you to identify the following factors which I will show you in a minute.

Jama's story

Jama is a 19 year old student who has being struggling for two years to pass her GCSE due to limiting thinking. I met Jama at my children's school. This young and polite girl, who lost her dad two years ago said she has never being able to achieve any good thing since she lost her father, she said even when she tries to read she is not able to concentrate. She said when she want to read some restrictive thinking comes to her mind, making her lack of concentration and failing her exams and limiting her from going forward. I asked Jama whether or not she will allow me to work with her? She answered yes and I took Jama on board.

First thing I ask Jama to do is to renew her mind and belief that she has the ability to achieve what ever she wants in life and that working together as a team she will pass her GCSE. After renewed her mind I told her to carefully study herself for the next two days, write down what things she avoid doing, what things consumes her energy, what things did she put aside even though she knows that she need to do them, and what thing gave poor results in her life for the two days and to bring the list with her when next she is coming to see me.

Jama did exactly as advised. Together we did another assessment where we both recognised that some activities are not necessary in achieving her GCSE and we both agreed that she should put them aside and focus on the important ones that we identified together. I helped Jama to formulate and design a plan of what she needs to do so that she can enjoy doing the necessary things. I and my team worked together with Jama for 1year and 3 months. Last year, this wonderful girl passed her GCSE with flying colours and will be going to the university this year.

The people I have worked with have come to realize the importance of creativity and passion. They understood that if these were lost in a business or in whatever they need to achieve, success would elude it. These people have discovered that there is a uniqueness approach to power and success. We have taught them to be receptive to others, and are encouraged to build relationships. They are taught to use their creativity to create win-win situations relying on their intuition to manifest opportunities. They know how to attract the result they desire for themselves and their future generations.

Kerry's story

Kerry is a 30years old, beautiful, clever and polite lady. She was pursuing a career in journalism when I met her. She told me how she has being contemplating on stopping from attending her lectures in the university. She said she has previously dropped out from the university on two different occasions studying two different courses. Kerry explained to me how for four years she avoided going back to the university as she constantly reminds herself of her previous failures. Firstly we made Kerry to understand that she is not a failure she just hasn't got it right yet. Then she began to belief in herself once again, and we worked with her step-by-step all through until she happily completed her degree in her choice of career and university.

Friend, at the end of each day, before going to bed, cultivates the habit of taking some time out to ask yourself about the following questions, which are the limiting thinking of the mind.

- What things did I "avoid, and refused to act upon today
- What things are energy consuming in my life today
- What things did I put aside or run away from doing today
- What things did I do and it gave a poor result in my life today and hated myself for doing it.

Once you have successfully identified these limiting thinking, I advice that you ask yourself **"out loud"** for example I will ask myself out loud (Abimbola, "are these things that I have always hated to do necessary or important to my success and my becoming a millionaire or successful") if my answer is yes then I will begin to find a way of enjoying what I need to do, and this is how.

For seven good days I will work on myself, I will determine to solve the problem by facing it squarely.

I will write down those things that are going on in the inside of me while I am doing these activities. I will then carefully look through what I have written down. This will give me an understanding of what needs to change and I will start developing a plan to change my limited thinking, but if my answer to the question is no then I will just literally drop all the things and not waste my time on them.

Concept 2: You need a good ATTITUDE:

What is attitude?

Attitude is a way of regarding or explaining a reaction. As a matter of fact, people either have a positive or a negative attitude. When our attitudes are positive that is fine and it may help us attain a lot of good things in life. However, if our attitudes are negative it is a problem which requires an urgent solution.

It is true that the power of a positive attitude has a way of attracting positive responses from life and from other people around us.

I call this experience "life changing" others call it "life rejoinder". In my many years of working with people to change their attitude, I have found that whenever people change their inner attitude and consciousness, life has a way of responding positively to them, compensating them and making them happy.

Life brings success, prospect, hope and joy to those who make this mental adjustment. I believe once you are continuous in your success plan and goals, it will soon manifest in your effort to have a financial freedom which will in turn make you a millionaire and successful.

Since our thinking affects all aspects of our life, it is important that we endeavour to listen to our inner mind constantly and this will help us to recognize our thoughts pattern and how they affect the way we react to live problems.

One thing I need to emphasize on is that, it is important to listen to our inner mind but it is more importantly that we tune down a negative voice as it is capable of affecting our behaviours in live. When you are stressed, you are more likely to have more negative thoughts so watch out.

Live is full of ups and downs, which can cause human being to become stressed. Research has proven that stress is not good as it triggers the release of some hormones in the body system. When these hormones are released frequently in the body, they can cause serious damages which could cause cardiovascular disease, cancer, liver problems and many more. The solution to this is to un-wine the stress regularly, either by swimming, sleeping at least 7 to 8 hours every night and taking a knap at regular intervals during the day. Sound sleep helps to improve and maintain high level of energy, good immune system, effective mental alertness, and emotional clarity and most importantly a good quality life.

My friend, before we go any further I will like to show you different types of attitude and how to send a mental correction to your mind in order to change a negative attitude into a positive one. There are four main types of attitudes which are

- Attitude about ourselves
- Attitude towards others and things around us
- Attitude towards life itself
- Attitude toward the environment we live in

What are the attitudes about ourselves, these are identified as having high or low self-esteem (self-esteem means good opinion of oneself), or having a high or low degree of self-confidence (self-confidence means having confidence in one's own abilities).

In order to actually become somebody in life, we must first learn how to believe totally in ourselves, we must have a very good opinion of ourselves and also belief in our own ability to achieve success and become a millionaire.

Beloved, if you don't believe in yourself nobody is ready to believe in you. Without believing in yourself, you will constantly send a negative signal to your mind thinking that you can not achieve the success required to be successful and to become a millionaire.

If you are one of the people with low self-esteem or low confidence, don't worry there is a solution to it.

I'm sure your next question is how, and what is the solution? It is simple and I will show you now.

WHAT IS THE SOLUTION TO LOW SELF-ESTEEM OR LOW CONFIDENCE?

All you have to do when you are feeling a low self esteem is

1. Put on a good music that can lift up your spirit.

2. Bring the feelings to your conscious mind (remember we have both conscious and unconscious mind) and deal with it there in your conscious mind by sending a reverse message such as the following:

   - Yes! I can do it in replacement of No I can not do it.
   - Yes! I have the ability to do whatever I want to do in replacement of No I do not have the ability to do what I need to do.
   - Yes! I have the ability to be successful in life.
   - Yes! I am capable of achieving my goals or what ever I set my mind on to achieve.
   - Yes! I have the ability to become a millionaire in replacement of I can not have a financial freedom.

You then need to send all these reverse versions back to your subconscious mind. Then make sure to magnetise it in your mind. You need to glue it there in your mind. Once your subconscious mind is able to accept the information, then sit back and watch what happens from that moment henceforth. Your subconscious mind will continue to send the positive information to your conscious mind and it will begin to reflect in your attitude towards yourself, others around you, the life and even your surroundings and environment.

3. Surround yourself with people who are capable of lifting you up not those that will talk you down.

WHAT TO DO WHEN YOU HAVE ATTITUDE ABOUT OTHER PEOPLE:

Attitude about others, this may include our good or bad feelings towards other people, our trust or mistrust of other people and many more. The simple fact is that if you have bad feelings about someone you can never be a true friend to them neither will you open your mind to them.

And who knows, that might be the person you need to know for your next breakthrough to manifest. They might be the ones to help you towards your achievement.

Do you know that keeping bad feelings in our mind can also affect our health tremendously? It can lead to cancer. Beloved, this is the last thing you want for yourself. I pray that you have a good health to enjoy your coming wealth.

Listen friend, if you have a bad feeling towards someone, I come to let you know that you can revolt against the feelings by doing the following:

1. By sending a positive message about the person to your subconscious mind (such as that guy is a nice man all I have to do is try and understand him better). Find one or two things which he has done nicely to you in the past and says to yourself continuously, I know he is a nice man; he has done this and that in the past. Therefore if he can do all those good things before then he can do much better, all I have to do is give him another chance, and be more patient with him.

2. By tolerating the person and extending your hand of love to him or her.

3. By extending a hand of friendship to the person

4. By overlooking peoples mistakes.

5. By forgiving people.

WHAT TO DO WHEN YOU HAVE ATTITUDE ABOUT LIFE:

Attitude about life include the feeling that good things will never come our ways, or that we are created to experience failures and difficulties. Attitude about life may manifest itself in either of two ways.

It is either positive expression such as:

- Ambitious
- Motivation
- Appreciative
- Aspiration
- Caring.
- Friendly
- Positive thinking.

OR

Negative expression such as:

- Self-satisfied.
- Unmotivated.
- Ungrateful.
- Resentful.
- Uncaring and many more.
- Self pitying.
- Carefree behaviour.
- Bad thinking.
- Wrong thinking.
- Negative thinking.

Friend, do you know that your attitude can attract things, objects, and good luck. Let me give you an example, I went shopping in the west end on this faithful day, bought a book in preparation for a business meeting in order to settle a business deal, on getting back to the car I realized I was given £1 over my change, but because I was rushing for the meeting I couldn't take the £1 back to the sales assistance. I got to the meeting quite alright but the boss of one of the big companies peeped out from the board room and said "I'm the director of this company, I'm sorry, but I'm not interested in the meeting anymore.

I felt so disappointed but on my way back home I stopped by and I returned the £1 coin to the attendant. Twenty minutes after I got home I checked my email and it was the same man who said to me that he doesn't want the meeting to go ahead who has emailed that they have decided that the contract should be given to my company.

You see that is the power of an improved attitude which attracted response from life.

A positive attitude is capable of leading you to your destiny and success. It can even make you become a millionaire.

HOW YOU CAN DEVELOP YOUR POSITIVE ATTITUDE

❖ Listen constantly to your inner thoughts and make sure to capture every negative thought and change them to positive ones. I.e. I can't do this should become I can do it wonderfully.

❖ When you communicate with people, communicate with positive words that will lift people's spirit up and not those that are capable of putting them down. Think before you speak, let people identify you with positive and motivational words only. Do not communicate with such words that could make people around you feel empty, hurt, frustrated, angry or less important. Never communicate in a harsh voice.

❖ Listen to good music, reconnect with your nice old friends, visit museums, listen to your 4 to 5years old talk, I bet they will make you laugh. Have a long walk out in the evenings and enjoy the fresh breeze. Spend some quality time on your own. Enjoy warm and relaxing bath; tell your kids night time stories and constantly read books that are of great interest to you.

❖ Invite friends to lunch with you and pay the bills.

❖ Help people in anyway you could.

❖ Love people and allow yourself to be loved.

❖ Look after your health.

❖ Exercise regularly, eat good balance diet.

❖ Create happy environment around yourself.

❖ Move with positive waves from positive people.

❖ Constantly create calming environment around you.

❖ Help people to find the potentials in them.

HOW WILL POSITIVE ATTITUDE MANIFEST ITSELF?

- Experiencing and expecting success.
- Be motivated until you achieve your goals.
- Happiness.
- Being inspired from inside yourself.
- Never give up; you are not a looser but a winner.
- Constructive thinking leading to positive actions.
- Creative thinking.
- Positive thinking.
- Ability to see opportunities and to grab them and do something with them.
- Seeing problems and failure as an opportunity to do better.
- Always see a bright side of life.
- Use positive affirmation regularly.

The following are hints to change a negative attitude into a positive one.

- Make the effort to understand any negative attitude about yourself, other people and life. Then come up with a plan to make them positive or otherwise change them for the better, and act your plan. For example, your plan may be to begin to see other people around you as blessings because nobody can live alone on earth. The earth is so massive we need other people before we can be able to enjoy it.
- Try and make the effort to have only positive thoughts and feelings throughout the day. Catch every small negative thought and neutralize it.
- Speak with positive minded people and people who believed in you and your ability to succeed.

Common Question from my clients is Do you think I can do these things and attain success?

My answer is always yes you can. All you need to do is to train yourself to recognise negative thoughts and then stop whatever you are doing and deal with it immediately.

Concept 3: Determination:

WHAT IS DETERMINATION?

According to Field et al (1998), self-determination is a combination of skills, knowledge, and beliefs that enable a person to engage in a goal-directed, self-regulated, autonomous behaviour. It is an understanding of one's strengths and limitations together with a belief in one's self as capable and affective which are essential to self-determination.

Beloved, when acting on the basis of these skills and attitudes, individuals have greater ability to take control of their lives and assume the role of successful and responsible adults particularly when dealing with businesses and making money.

Do you know that in order to gain control over your life you need to take some actions which only you can take for yourself? No one is able to take such decisions for you.

These actions involve learning and applying a number of skills such as finding information, setting goals, understanding your strengths and inabilities to achieve your goal, your problem-solving skill, and yourself belief.

Self determination will move you from your dream to being able to achieve the reality of the dream and become a successful person. This world is full of so many distractions but self-determination is the only route to your success.

Success is defined as possessing the capability for self-determination.

Friend, self-determination is the ability to decide what you want to do with your life and then take actions on that decision and make sure that you do not stop acting until you achieve what you have determined and have set out your mind to achieve.

I know the next question is how then do I self-determine? It's easy and I will show you how

With self-determination comes success. A proverb says "Determination determines destiny" in other words, once you determine to attain a certain level of success in your life you immediately become unstoppable, I mean nothing can stop you because without realising it your mind will automatically begin to design a road map which will get you to where you have determined to get to.

The first thing is to make up your mind whether you want that particular thing or not. If your mind is in a doubt, with the feelings of uncertainty, you will not be able to make your mind up. Do you know that not being able to make up your mind in itself can be a blockage to your success?

Do you also know that the moment you are unable to make up your mind the problem begins, because you would not be able to make any plan or move forward? Therefore it is mandatory for you to make up your mind today and start doing what you need to do (remember millionaires make up their minds quickly, take decisions on the issue at hand and act on it immediately).

Concept 4: Focus:

What does it mean to be focused?

FOCUS means to concentrate on something. It means a centre of interest. Once you are self-determined and you know what you want the next thing is to focus on that which you have identified.

How do I focus? I will tell you and this is how!

Begin, by making a complete and accurate assessment of your potential with regards to that which you have identified and determined to do, for example if I have decided and self-determined to manufacture a glass, I will make a complete assessment of my ability to successfully manufacture the glass. To do this

- I will take an inventory of myself.

- I will make a few lists concerning this decision.
- I will make a list of these things involved in making a glass
- I will sit down and make a list of all the things I can do well concerning glass making.
- I will list those things I can not do well when it comes to glass manufacturing.
- I will make sure I'm honest with myself when writing these lists
- From my list of things involved in making a glass, I will make a list of all the things I like to do, even if they are things I think I can not do (this is because I know I can work on my thinking.)
- Then I will make a list of all the things I would like to do, if I
- could do them.
- Finally I will list all my hobbies and incorporate them into my list so that I can enjoy every step all the way through to manufacturing my glass.

However, for me to be able to move forward and do what I have determined to do I have to shut off that voice in my head saying I can not manufacture a glass, and also ignore the voices of negative people around me telling me manufacturing a glass is impossible.

Mentally and subconsciously, I will replace the voice of stagnancy with what I call the "voice of encouragement" such as Abimbola, you can do it, you can manufacture a glass, and it is possible, go for it, start now, and start immediately. This is where I need to act to be my own best friend.

It amazing how much forgiving and charitable we are with our friends, families and neighbour than we are with ourselves. If I have ever failed in manufacturing something before I will deal with it now, I will forgive myself for having being unable to complete the manufacturing tasks the last time.

Next I will go to the list of things I like to do but feel I can not do well. Speaking as my own best friend, I will ask myself if I think there are some things on this list that could be moved to my list of things I can do well. And I will treat my hobby list in the same manner. I will do the same thing to all the lists.

Next I will go to the list of things I would like to do but which I couldn't do and I will ask myself why can't I do this, and I will put my reasons on another list. Friend, I'm sure you will begin to say in your mind "What is it about all these lists?" Well, I have just successfully made an assessment of myself.

This is a way you could assess yourself if you would like to.

Right, this is where we are going. If you look over my lists you will find out that I was not focusing on all the things I feel I can not do and the reason why I can not do them (I call these limitation lists, they are negative thoughts), rather I should focus on my potentials. Therefore friend, you need to focus yourself more on the things you can do well, and figure out how you can start doing them immediately.

I will urge you not to focus on what "You can not do" but focus on "your potentials and can do well".

For instance, if you like to play basketball but you think you are not tall and so you don't even try. In this case, you are looking at it from the point of your limitations. Now try and look at it from another angle, from your strengths, you can say, although I may not be tall and bulky but I can handle how to play basketball well, I have the stamina to do it.

I can't change my being short, but I can refuse to let my being short overcome my strengths. Hence I will move forward, I will try my hands on it, and then take some actions. If I need training I will go for training.

If I need more information I will look for it everywhere and anywhere including on the internet.

Veronica's story

Veronica is a 40 years old lady whose dream is to become a midwife right from her youth but always have a feeling behind her mind that she could not become one. She said she started a nursing course in 2004 but she stopped as she couldn't see herself fulfilling that dream. I met veronica four years ago and started working with her, a year later she gained an admission into the school of nursing and midwifery. She was taught how to self determine and to follow through. She is doing her final year now. Well done Veronica keep focused and keep going.

Concept 5: You need to be able to follow through:

WHAT IS TO FOLLOW THROUGH?

Before we can follow through we need to write a plan of action which we will follow through. That's right I will discuss that fully in chapter two and I will show you how to write a plan of action. Basically, following through means to develop a plan to reach your targeted goal and then follow it step by step until you hit your target, win and become a millionaire.

CHAPTER TWO

Six IMPORTANT STEPS TO MAKE YOUR DREAM A REALITY:

Step 1: Visualization: seeing your product in your thought.

What is Visualization?

Visualization is all about seeing yourself at the other end of the passageway before you start acting your plan. People who become millionaires are those who believe that they will make it regardless. There are many reasons why many people fail to achieve their goals and a small percentage of people do achieved theirs, this is because not many people believe in their ability to be successful. In order to achieve one's goals, the following must be in place.

1. The prospect millionaire must visualize a plan for his or herself

2. Must develop a plan of action

3. Must have the inner urge to make point one and two work.

Do you know that everything starts with a dream? Without a dream nothing happens. Do you also know that the chair you are sitting on started with someone's dream, and so were the clothes you are wearing this very moment.

Nonetheless, there is a difference between dreaming and visualizing. Brother and sister, do you know that before you start what ever you want to do, you must visualize yourself succeeding on that which you are about to start? In other words you must be able to see the finished product before you even start it.

My brother and sister, we need to solidify our goals into our thinking so as to indicate the true worth of their achievement. People need to visualize the feeling they will experience when coming into the finishing line of the goal. Visualization really does put you in the picture. You are able to see what is yet to happen. Visualization is defined as "Bringing something as a picture before the mind". Someone says if you can see it then it becomes more credible. In other words, if you can't see it you can't have it.

Brother and sister, are you with me, are you starting to see what the power of visualization is all about and how it can work for you? if you can see what it is that you wanted, then you are half done, all you need to do then is to design the course to get you there. Do you know that often our visualization is carried out sub-consciously?

What is the importance or benefits of visualization to becoming a millionaire?

- It helps you to see yourself in your wealth.
- It helps you work through your plan of become a millionaire.
- It helps to keep you going during the times of difficulties.

- It gives you the happiness and joy before you make the money.
- It allows you to think like a winner and a successful person.

Carolyn's Story

Carolyn is a 41year old single lady who found it difficult to get a relationship going. She said she is yet to get married because she has not yet come across anybody who wants to settle down with her. Carolyn was at the point of committing suicide when I bumped into her at a corner shop. She was very tearful and I was moved to give her tissue paper, a shoulder to cry on and to ask what the problems are.

Since her situation requires an urgent solution, I introduced myself to Carolyn and told her what I do. I asked if she would like to meet with me for a brief interview/discussion. She agreed and I took her cell number, called and gave her my earliest available appointment. After a brief discussion with my client I realised she had lost hope in herself, she said life does not worth living.

Firstly, we worked very hard to re-install back self confidence in Carolyn and she was taught on how to constantly visualize a healthy and long lasting relationship, I taught her how to belief and have hope in herself. Then I advised her about how to magnetise and keep a good relationship. My team and I taught Carolyn that the starting point of a good relationship is to belief that good and healthy friendships are created when people belief that those differences make people and life interesting and better to endure.

We taught her those lasting relationships are those based on unconditional love and sharing. People need to tolerate each other and see their partners as life partners. Carolyn was made to understand how to become selfless, make her partner comfortable, relaxed and happy, whenever they are together.

Carolyn was also taught about the magic of sacrificing for the sake of love. Both partners in a relationship have to sacrifice for each other. They need to bend their rules to accommodate their partners.

Secondly, she was advised on how to deal with confusions, problems or misunderstanding as soon as they comes up, and never to leave misunderstanding unresolved for too long as it could escalate, become unsolvable and could even end the relationship.

Communication plays a big role in healthy relationships. Partners should be able to listen, share and express their feelings with each other.

There are no doubt that their will be differences in personality, and behaviours, rather than expect your partner's personality to change, it is wise to work on their behaviours. All you can do with personality is to try and understand your partner's personality.

Step 2: Setting goals

What is Goal Setting?

Goal setting is a standard technique used by millionaires and achievers all over the world. It gives the setter long-term vision and short-term motivation. It also focuses the setter's attainment of knowledge and helps him or her to organize his or her resources in order to achieve a good outcome.

May I emphasize the importance of setting a goal? Do you know that by setting, clear and defined goals, you can measure and take pride in the achievement of those goals? Do you also realise that you can see forward progress in what might previously have seems a long pointless defeat.

Goal setting raises your self-confidence as you recognize your ability and competence in achieving the goals that you have set. Now that we can see how much goal setting can benefit our lives we will then proceed to what tools we need to set the goals.

I'll show you different levels involved in a millionaire's goal setting which are laid out as follows:-

Decide what you want to do with your financial life and what large-scale goals you want to achieve in your lifetime. Then break these goals down into smaller and smaller targets that you need to hit so that you are able to reach your lifetime goal. Once you have your plans, then you start working towards achieving them.

To give a broad balanced coverage of all important areas in life, I will advice that we set goals in all different areas of life.

1. Financial goals:
    Write down clearly how much you want to earn by what stage and at what age and on what date, i.e. ten million in five years time.

2. Physical goals:
    Write down what you want to achieve in order to have good health deep into your old age. State what steps you are going to take to achieve it

3. Pleasure goals
    Write down clearly how you want to enjoy yourself, make sure that some of your life is yours. Enjoy life.

Friend, once you have classified your goals in the above categories, assign a priority to them in which ever way you like. Also ensure that the goals you have set are the goals you want to achieve, not what someone else wants them to be.

The next step is to set a 10 year plan of smaller goals that you will need to complete if you are to reach your lifetime plan. Then set a 5 year plan, 1 year plan, 6 month plan, 1 month, 1 week plan, and daily plans. Now start following gradually those progressively smaller goals that you should reach to achieve your lifetime goals.

Each of these should be based on the previous plan. It is important to review the plans regularly in order to make sure that they fit the way in which you want to live your life.

I'm sure the next thing going in your mind is how do I set a sensible goal? I'll tell you

*I*n setting a sensible goal you need to follow a guideline. How do I follow a guideline? I don't even know what guidelines are anyway. It's easy and I will explain it to you. This is how it works: you need to set **a PCGVA** goal.

So what is a PCGVA goal?

PCGVA means your goal should be **precise, criterion, get- done, valuable** and **appropriate.**

The key force that either drives you toward your goal or holds you back is your subconscious mind. Those guidelines are the necessary criteria for your subconscious mind to accept your goals and start working for you. Otherwise it will work hard to keep you in the comfort zone of your present condition and which is not necessarily the best for you.

My friend, your chance of becoming a millionaire is **now.** Not next time, not tomorrow or next month but **now.** You just need to apply all these principles you are learning as you are reading this book and your life will never be the same again. Your goal needs to be exact, of good standard, accomplishable, worthwhile and have a finishing time.

Exact, simply means to write the goals down, which is crucial in all goal setting steps. The trick here is that the more definite your goal is, the more realistic your success will be, and the shorter the path leading you into it. Do you know that when you make your goals exact, you have already programmed your subconscious mind to work for you? Then your feelings and thoughts will lead you to your goals instead of pointing at the obstacles. To make your goals exact you also need to work out the other components of ESAWO goal setting guidelines, let's look at the S which means standard.

Standard simply means you must create a way of checking the progress you are making and these will allow you to know, and tell you to stop when the goal is achieved. Do you know that feeling and seeing the progress you are making is very important for you to stay motivated and enjoy the process of achieving your goal? The next one is A which means Accomplishable.

Accomplishable means you need to set a goal that you will see a realistic path to its achievement, and reasonable odds that you will get there. This does not mean that the lower you aim the more likely you reach success. It is well known that goals that work best also have a challenge in them. These types of goals will give the setter more motivation and sense of achievement. Let's look into the meaning of W (worthwhile).

Worthwhile means a goal is worth the pain. When you have clear reasons why you want to reach that goal. This is one more reason where it is important that the goal is really yours. Make sure to put your exact reasons and expected reward in writing. If possible, drawn some pictures to remind you of where you are going. The last alphabet is O which stands for Opportune.

Opportunity simply means the finishing time. It means that your goal should have a time limit. This is very important for your subconscious mind to work in your favour. Besides, time is part of the price you pay for the reward from achieving a goal. Setting the deadline will protect you from paying higher price than the goal is worth. This is also your protection from procrastination and perfectionism. Procrastination means pushing the starting point forward such as (I'll start tomorrow, oh I'll start next month and more, and they will never actually start). Finally, my brother and sister remember that millionaire goal setting is an important way of

- Deciding what and how much money you need to achieve in your life.
- Separate your money making goal from what is irrelevant to you.
- Motivating yourself to achieve the amount of money you want.
- Building yourself-confidence based on measured achievement of goals

*S*tep 3: Plan of action:

*W*hat is Plan of Action?

*A*n action plan is a list of tasks that the millionaire-to-be have to carry out in order to achieve an objective (i.e. becoming a millionaire). It focuses on the achievement of a single goal. Whenever you want to achieve something, draw up an action plan.

This will allow you to concentrate on the stages of that achievement and will keep you motivated all through.

In other words, it means a list of things that you need to do in order to achieve a goal. To use it, simply carry out each task in the list one after the other until you reach the last one, and that means you have achieved your goal.

At This Point, I Will Advice You That You Put the Book Down and Try to Recap on All You Have Learnt So Far

Make Yourself A Cup Of Coffee While You Are Recapping.

Now Check Your Clock, Is It Twenty Minutes Yet? If Yes Then You Can Pick Up The Book And Continue Reading.

Step 4: Starting day and time:

This goes hand in hand with step three above.

What is Starting day and Time?

Friend, in your plan of action you must state clearly what day to kick start the goal and what exact time to begin, and you must make sure to stick to whatever you have written down. You much do whatever it takes for you to get started. **"Remember a work never started is a work never finished".**

Speak to your subconscious mind that you need to get started. There is a common saying that **"If it is to be, it is up to me"**. In other words if I am to become a millionaire it is up to me, it is about what action I take daily.

Step 5: Check and make sure you start on the committed date:

Again this is the continuation of step 4. I can not stop laying emphasis on the importance of committing yourself to a commencement day and adhere to the commitment. Remember you need to have interest in what you want to do. If the power of your interest and desires are strong enough, nothing you have to do in order for you to achieve your goal will feel difficult to you. **Remember success needs action, not passivity!** (Passivity means not active).

Step 6: Create new ideas:

The most important thing in this step is to find a problem and determine to solve the problem. Then you **Brainstorm**. When you want to brainstorm you simply write down as much as you can in relation to the objectives outlined. Don't worry about strategic planning or anything like that yet. Just concentrate solely on idea generation.

Before you start brainstorming, make sure that you are at your peak state of mind and instruct your subconscious mind that it must do some serious **"Thinking"** trust me honey, I have been able to move mountains after very healthy brainstorming sessions. The next thing is to **focus on what you want.**

In order to give your idea the best chance to find the solution you will need to switch off from outside distractions.

Remember to tolerate nothing. Eradicate the distractions, the daily frustrations and pity party dramas of your life once and for all. Please do not just fix the problem. Re-design your routine so that the problem and irritations will never trouble you again.

Chapter Three

Five ideas of what to do

*I*dea 1: Start a business:

In our journey to becoming a millionaire, do you know that the most important key is investment? Starting your own business is the solution, so that you can be able to pay yourself any amount of wage you think you deserve. And not allow some employer somewhere to tell you your worth. Let's talk common sense here brother and sister do you know that the highest percentage of people all over the world rely on monthly pay-checks from their job, yet most of these people are wishing that they will one day become millionaires. Well I'm not sure if that can ever be possible.

Do you know that **J.O.B** means **Just Over Broke!** It is difficult to become a millionaire from earning monthly salary.

How then do I start a business? I will tell you.

Starting a business can be quit daunting but very rewarding too. Although there is no way to completely eliminate those risks involved but careful planning and research can improve your chances of becoming successful and making a good profit

So How Do I Start a Business!

However, in addition to what you will read under this section, I also advised that you seek professional help and advice before setting up your own business, God bless you.

*I*n starting your own business you need to consider your starting up strategies. Sit down and think about it over and over again, then make up your mind and take a decision about it. After taking your decision, write down your plan of action, commit yourself to your plan, and determine to follow it through.

*I*n your marketing strategies, you need a proven marketing system. It does not have to be one that is expensive but one that gives results. It should be effective and should be able to give your business your desired profit. Your marketing strategies should be able to communicate good things about you and your business in a way that will get customers doing business with you. The follow are important in a good marketing strategies.

- You must target the right customer.
- You must know the customer's need.
- Make sure that your customers know about your product and service.
- You must communicate your business and its missions clearly.
- Set realistic plans.
- You must understand every thing written in your plan.

- Constantly think about how to add value to your product.
- Aspire to get at least 40 new and loyal customer monthly.
- You must invest in yourself. Learn how to master marketing from the scratch.

Before starting your business it is important that you first assess your skills to find out whether or not you have all the necessary skills to operate a successful business. You are assessing yourself for drives, determinations, initiatives, motivation, mental and physical energy you need to start your business. In addition to the above, you are also assessing yourself for communication skills, managerial skills, creative skills, decision making skills and your ability to cope under stress.

The next thing is to develop your business idea into a viable, commercial product or service. This is a crucial stage in building a business. It is very important to create a **business plan.** A business plan is the soul of a successful business. If you are not sure of writing a business plan then do not hesitate to get help from the professionals. Remember there are people out there who will help you to set up your business.

*R*emember also to choose a name for your business. It is worth spending some time choosing a name for your business. It is one thing that your customers will notice about you. Therefore it is important to choose a name that gets the right message across to your customers now and in the future. You must also make sure that your workplace meets minimum standards under health and safety law.

HINT: Do you know that you can turn information to wealth? You can turn your ideas into saleable products and services that others really want and need, and are willing to pay you for. Wealth is generous, abundant and available for everyone, regardless of your age or gender. The only boundary and blocks are those created by you based on your thoughts beliefs and procrastination.

How can you advertise your business?

You need to advertise in other to get customers that will make you profit. One important thing you need to know is that advertising doesn't need to be expensive. And you need to identify your customers in order to advertise to the right people. There are many different types of advertising you can use, such as **customer getting you another customer:** this method simply means that if you have customers who are satisfied with your product or services, they will recruit more customers for you but you will offer them a reward.

Internet advertising is getting more and more popular these days. You can use pay per click on the search engine as a method of advertising where by you use the pay per click to get customers to your website. However, you need to know what you are doing with this method. You can invest on yourself in order to find out. You can use your **local community:** this method allows you to get your local post office put your advert paper through people's letter boxes and can also print flyers which you can get people to distribute for you and then you give them some money for doing so. Although you can advertise on radios and TV but these methods are very expensive.

How you can market your business

You can achieve the following marketing strategies free of charge

Industry events: a good entrepreneur will look out for his or her industry's events and offer to give free training and seminars. Through this way you will be known as an expert in your industry. **Flyers and leaflets** you can prepare a simply eye catching and mind moving flyers on your computer, which you can hand delivered to homes and businesses in your local area and even throughout your borough, district or region. **Business cards:** you should have a business card which not only have your basic details on them but also your sales messages. Do you know that you can print on both sides of your card? Use the maximum space available to you. **Press releases:** you must share things about your new products and services with your industry as well as the whole business world. Press release is easy to prepare, you can prepare one by yourself, all you need to do is go on the internet and check on some of the press release sites for ideas on structuring. If you prepare a newsworthy, mind sinking and interesting press release, the editors of newspapers and magazines as well as journalists are always on the lookout for interesting stories. You will be noticed, trust me, you will.

*I*dea 2: Invest your money on funds:

*I*nvest on money market fund.

*W*hat is money market fund?

*R*elax and I'll tell you

*M*oney market funds simply mean a low-risk mutual fund. These types of fund are relatively safe because they invest in a very short-term and high-quality type of bonds. The period between the issuance of the bonds and the dates is so short that these bonds usually don't fluctuate with regards to interest rates rise and fall.

Because the bond is issued by the institutional governments and financially secured companies helps reduce the risk. It is worth knowing that although the money market funds are a safe investment, it is important to known that these market funds are not insured by the Federal Deposit Insurance Corporation like bank money market accounts are.

Do you also know that money market funds make the risk worth your while by offering a better interest on the money you deposit, usually a few percentage point better than a savings account. I'm sure the next question is what are the advantages of money market funds? I'll tell you.

*T*he advantages include:

❖ Favourable interest rate. (These accounts are very useful if you have more than £1000 that you don't want to touch for a while, at least between 3 and 6 months).

❖ These funds pay a higher rate of interest than saving account. (Do you know that money that sits in a regular bank account often lose some interest even though it's hardly noticeable to you)?

❖ Many money market funds offer other perks and conveniences such as privileges so that you can have access to your money when you need it.

*I*dea 3: Re-invest your profits:

*B*efore you start investing your profits, do you know that you should have a goal? You should decide exactly what you are investing for. Most people invest because they are:

❖ Saving for when they can no longer work
❖ Saving because of the children's needs and education
❖ Saving for a down payment on a buy-to-let home
❖ Saving for a family holiday abroad
❖ Or saving to become a millionaire

*N*ow that you know your personal reasons for your investment, the question is what types of investments are out there for you to invest your profits in?

*T*here are different types of investments, which includes **Stock, Bonds, Money market bonds, Mutual funds** and **Variable annuities.**

*S*tocks: A stock share represents a small piece of a company. In other words the investment depends on how the company is doing. The investment increases or decreases in value based on the corporation's growth and profit.

Stocks are also called **equities,** and they are of high risk but at the same time they have the potential to produce high turn over.

*B*onds or fixed income security is a loan which an investor makes to the municipality, or government. In this case the bondholders do not own the entities that were issued on the bond. But bondholders are entitled to payments on the bonds.

The value of bonds fluctuates, therefore investors who trade bonds need to buy and sell the bonds before the maturity date otherwise they will not be able to make money due to their fluctuating value. However, holistically speaking bonds are less risky investments than the stocks, but you can only make money on them when left over a period of time.

*M*oney market funds: this was already discussed under idea 2 (Invest your money on funds).

*M*utual funds: they are also referred to as funds. They invest in dozens of individual stocks or bonds or on both. Mutual funds are run by a professional. A fund is owned by many individual investors who want their money to get access to investments they were not able to manage on their own.

*V*ariable annuities (**VA**) are similar to mutual funds they both invest in a bunch of individual stocks and bonds through different single investors.

Variable annuities are similar to insurance product because if the investor dies, the spouse continues to receive VA income payment. The next of kin usually receive the money as was put into the account after reduction of any early withdrawals and applicable fees.

Although majority of wealthy people inherited their wealth but that does not mean that you can not single out and become a self made millionaire. All you need to do is to focus on investment and accumulation and also to train your children how to invest and accumulate.

Investment is a choice; it is a means by which an individual is ready to take risk by saving his or her hard earn money with the hope to gain. To succeed in investment you need to be clear about Business Management.

Management in business is a means by which an individual gather people together to accomplish desire goals. Management comprises of planning, organizing, staffing, leading and controlling an organization.

The Functions of management includes:

- *Planning:- You need to have a vision of what will happen in your business in the future*
- *Organization: - You need to be able to use your available resources to enable the success of your business.*
- *Staffing: - You need to analyse jobs, evaluate recruitment, and hiring the right individual to the right jobs.*

- *Leading/ motivating: - You need to exhibit leadership and motivational skills.*
- *Monitoring: - You must be able to regularly monitor, and check progress against plan.*

You need to formulate a business policy which needs to include:

- ❖ *The mission of your business*
- ❖ *The vision of your business*
- ❖ *The objective of your business*
- ❖ *The strategy you intend to use in coordinating your plan of action.*

You also need a business process management. This means a field of management focused on aligning organizations with the wants and needs of the customer. It is known as a holistic management approach. This method promotes business effectiveness and efficiency while striving for innovation, flexibility and integration with technology.

Business process can also be associated with collection of related, structured activities that meet the need of the customer. Business process is as traditional as concepts of task.

*I*dea 4: Find a problem and solve it:

Friend, do you know that making other people's problems your concern and trying to solve the problem is a good idea? Do you also know that people are willing to pay you for whatever problem you are able to solve? I'm sure you will be thinking in your mind (what is my business with other people's problems when I've got enough of mine).

Well there is joy and reward in solving other people's problems.

*T*he next question will be how do I solve problems then? Well I'll tell you. There are different strategies involved in problem solving and I will discuss some of them in the next section. First and foremost, In order for you to be able to solve a problem you need to understand the problem.

*T*he first step is to **Clarify the problem**. Brother and sister, it is easier to solve a problem if it is specific and clear, therefore it is important to understand the problem.

After understanding the problem, the next stage is to **know the main factors of the problem.** We need to find out the main elements of the problem before we can start looking for a solution (for example, if a 9 year old cries whenever you send him to bed) you need to find time to sit him down and ask him why he cries every night when he is going to bed.

The next strategy is to **Picture the problem,** see the problem in your inner mind. For examples, if you want to go and fetch water from a well and you think it is a problem, then try to see the picture of what you want to do first, see how you will walk to the well, also make a picture of how you will draw the water and put the bucket on your head and walk back to your house.

Another strategy is to *d*raw **a picture of the problem,** for example if you want to run a mile, draw a diagram showing the process involved in running.

The final one is **to *C*onsider the levels and systems,** for example if we want to prevent a disease we should consider events that trigger the disease at the level of the external environment.

*I*dea 5: Be ready to help people:

It is important to remember the needy as you are progressing on your way to becoming a millionaire.

*T*ry and light other people's candles as you are moving forward in your journey. Remember your candle loses nothing by lighting other people's candles. Try to help those people that have no means of helping you in return. Beloved, then sit back and watch how nature will turn round and begin to help you.

Take some of the needy along with you as you are climbing your success ladder and see how God himself will see you through your millionaire goals. Friends feed and shelter the needy and God will not forget you

CHAPTER FOUR

FIVE LAWS TO KEEP YOUR CUSTOMERS

*L*aw 1: Put your customers first:

*I*n whichever business you do, it is important to put your customers first, because your business can not survive without people patronising you, therefore try to make your customers happy. The question is how can I keep my customers first and make them happy? It's easy and I will tell you.

There are some steps involved in making your customers happy. What ever the type of product or service we supply, it is imperative that you always put our customers first. If a customer is dissatisfied with your product or service, they will stop doing business with your company, and even worse, they are likely to express their discontent to at least seven other people. That is a whole lot of bad publicity.

*A*nother hint is to answer customer's telephone by the third ring, promptly and politely answer their question, and providing quality goods and services

*L*aw 2: Listen to the customer's complaint: (2Cs)

One good way to deal with this aspect in order to satisfy your customer is to remember that most loyal customers are always the ones who had an adequately solved problem, rather than those who never had a problem. In order to be able to deal with a complaint satisfactorily, you need to find out what is it that makes that customer unhappy and deal with it as best as you can, making sure that the customer is happy with your solution.

Remember that discovering the problem provides an insight on possible solutions to the problem. Do you know that some problems can be alleviated through the implementation of a "partnership approach with the customer"?

The question is how do I form partnerships with a difficult customer? It's easy and I'll tell you.

*F*orming partnership with the customer requires the ability to find a common and mutual respect for one another which is imperative. In order to initiate this procedure, it is important to find out about the true complaint that the customer has and look for the best way to solve it, because we should be willing to listen to people's needs before trying to provide them with a solution.

In other words, if we are not willing to listen, how can we truly understand what is going to suit the individual's needs? Partnership is mainly about listening and avoiding assumptions that the problem always lies with the other party.

The next step is to **provide solutions.** With a strong understanding of what ails the customer, investigate what the customer thinks will provide a solution to the problem. However keep in mind that the key to providing solution is to avoid arguments, and remember that customers are always right.

*B*e consistent, remember consistency demands respect while inconsistency only leads to excuses. One important aspect of being consistent is by following through with promises. And finally, take responsibility for your actions. This includes doing as promised when you abated, and always follow up after working to solve a problem and ensure the customer's satisfaction. Doing this will convince your customer of a true level of commitment to the relationship.

*L*aw 3: Respect your customer:

It is important to respect and regard your customers. Please take this on board.

*L*aw 4: Provide high quality product/services:

Make sure your product and services are of high quality, and make the customer understand these too. In your marketing communications, you need to let your customers know the benefits your business has for them and you need to make these benefits as specific as possible. You need to stress what the prospects will get when they use your product/service. You need to add credibility to your argument by telling them what others have achieved with your product/service. These testimonial need to be specific and they need to be specifically attributed.

You need to provide an offer or immediate action. Brother and sister remember it is your job to stress the benefits and provide an offer that gets the prospect to act quickly to acquire them.

CHAPTER FIVE

THREE ACTIONS TO KEEP YOUR BUSINESS EXPANDING:

Before I start discussing the ways, I will stress that you make **"Marketing a priority"** commit to making time and make some money available for marketing whether to attend networking events or put together a brochure and research prospects on the Web or write a proposal.

Friend, you need to **cultivate positive thinking.** Negative emotions like worry, frustration and anxiety can only do one thing which is to waste time and cause you to panic. It is hard to market your products or services when you're stuck in panic mode. Use the system I will tell you now to benefit from worries.

The trick is that when things don't go according to plan stop and ask yourself **"What can I learn from this situation that will push me closer to my goals and my breakthrough"?** Call your name out loud and ask yourself what can I do now to make today more successful despite the setback? Say no anxiety and "prescript" worries into proactive and positive thoughts.

*A*ction 1: Improve your product:

It is important to offer something of value to your current customers. In order to differentiate your product or service, it is necessary to provide a benefit that your competitors do not have or produce. This will give you an edge over your competitors. It will make your customers always want to buy from you.

Beloved, do you know that the key to improving and differentiating a product or service is the identification and delivery of an important benefit that is not currently available in the market? Successful improvement and differentiation of a product or service start with an in-depth understanding of buyer purchase logic.

What is purchase compulsive?

*P*urchase compulsive is the description of how and why someone buys a particular product. You need to know what an individual customer wants and why that person sorts your product among all the other different ones in the market.

In order to improve our service or product, we must first understand how and why someone buys that kind of product or service, as well as ours in particular.

We need to find out what benefit they are seeking, and what benefits they actually obtain from the product. A clear understanding of our market's needs and wants, and their relative importance will give us the guidance we require to make effective changes that improve and differentiate our offering from that of our competitors.

*A*ction 2: Know your competitors and the market:

Brother and sister, before you start any business, it is important to carry out a market research. I'm sure the question will be **what is a market research?**

A market research is a systematic, objective collection and analysis of data about your target market, competitor, and the environment with the goal being increased understanding.

Another question probably may be what will my business benefit from the market research? Well there are a lot of benefits from a market research and some of them are as follows:

- ❖ Information gained from marketing research can guide your strategic business decisions.
- ❖ It can guide your communication with current and potential customers. (In what way?) Well once you have a good research, you should be able to formulate a more effective and targeted marketing campaigns that speak directly to the people you're trying to reach in a way that interests them.
- ❖ It helps you to identify opportunities in the marketplace
- ❖ Market research minimizes the risk of doing business. (for example the result of market research may indicate that you should not pursue a planned course of action)
- ❖ Another benefit is that the information gathered through market research helps you to determine if you're reaching your goals.

*A*ction 3: Make sure you are not charging too high or too little for your product/ services:

BEYOND MILLIONAIRE'S THINKING

It is important to charge whatever you think your product or service is worth but you must make sure that you are not over charging your customers because this is a strong factor that could affect your relationship with the client.

Another way you can do this is to charge what ever you think the client is able to pay. If your business is a small/new business it is going to be on a pretty tight budget. Larger companies can normally afford to pay more.

A millionaire to be must have the following characteristics:

- ❖ Must be willing to start his or her or own business
- ❖ Must be ready to take risks
- ❖ Must be ready to solve problems
- ❖ Must be willing to lead while others follow
- ❖ Must be able to lead a team

Do you know that a millionaire to be must also have what I call the 3Ds?

- Determination
- Devotion
- Direction

Advantages of becoming a millionaire are as follows

- ❖ You will have financial freedom
- ❖ You will have time freedom
- ❖ No boss to tell you what to do
- ❖ You will have enough money to help the needy.

CHAPTER SIX

Three Principles you need in order to make Real Estate your fast train to becoming a millionaire:

Principle 1: You need to make up your mind to use Real Estate to become a millionaire.

What is Real Estate?

Real Estate means mainly properties. This includes

- Residential real estate
- Commercial real estate
- Raw land
- Farm land

These four should be fine at the moment, because I don't want you to be confused. For a starter, I will show you how to achieve your aim with single family homes, normally referred to as flats, semi-detached or detached houses.

The main one we are using for this achievement is the Residential real estate. This type of real estate is divided into three different units which are as follows:

- Single family houses
- Small multi unit properties
- Condominium

*P*rinciple 2: Let me take you through the simple route of achieving your success through real estate.

Now, I assume you have made up your mind to be successful and want to make your wealth through real estate.

So the first thing you should be thinking about right this moment is **"How do I find a reasonably priced property?** Remember we are using Single Family houses to achieve our purpose.

Relax and I will tell you. Beloved, the first key to finding a good priced property is to develop the ability to identify and recognize owners who wants to sell urgently due to one reason or the other.

In order to identify this type of sellers, particularly if you are using the advert, you need to look for things like

- We are anxious to sell this property as we are old
- We are flexible to interested buyers
- We are moving out of this Country
- We need to sell as soon as possible
- We can't keep this property
- We need a smaller property as we can't avoid this one any more

When you have placed the right advert and get the right sellers you will be able to sense in your spirit that these people have a problem such as, they might need to sell because they are being transferred therefore they must sell. It might be that they are going through a divorce and therefore they must sell. It might even be a problem such as serious illness. It might be that they are migrating to another area. Whatever it is you will be able to sense a problem.

Friend, now that you know what a good priced property is, I need to show you how you can find them.

How Can I find a good priced Property?

- You need to place classified adverts and property adverts in shops, newspaper and magazine.
- You need to search through the computer (i.e. rightmove. com)
- You can also use leaflets, flyers and business cards to achieve these.
- You can use referrals method such as friends and families or neighbour.
- You can also drive around to look for reasonably priced houses.

Let's now assume that you have found a good bargain, the next thing is to sit down and look into the properties you have found and choose which one is the best out of them all.

The next thing is to contact the sellers either personally or by writing a letter. I will advise you to write a letter so that it can look professional and you have a written document

HINT:

Never look desperate if you go in to the seller or sound anxious in your letter to the seller if you have decided to write one.

The next thing is to talk about the price, tell the seller what you can avoid. If the seller agree with you and you are satisfied with the price, then get your lawyer involved and the rest will be history.

*P*rinciple 3: Determine to do what you were taught in this book and the sky is the limit for your success.

Friend, you need to put all you have learnt into practise. Remember if you do not act you can not have. I believe in you, I know you can do it therefore believe in yourself and start doing what you need to do today.

Wealth knows no limit, there are no boundaries to how wealthy one can become, the more wealth you make the more you can use it to attract more. Wealth is in abundance, there are room for everyone to become a millionaire through regular investment. Everyone has the potential to retire as a millionaire. Everyone also has the potential to create streams of income for themselves. There is no shortage of money; everyone that wants it can enjoy money in abundance.

CHAPTER SEVEN

CHANGE FOR BETTER

Change from being selfish to

- ➢ Being generous.
- ➢ Being kind.
- ➢ Being liberal.
- ➢ Being munificent.
- ➢ Be giving.
- ➢ Be opened handed.
- ➢ Have a big heart.
- ➢ Being philanthropic.
- ➢ Being bountiful.
- ➢ Being unsparing.
- ➢ Being unstinting.

Change from being egoistic to

- ❖ Being altruism.
- ❖ Being unselfish.

❖ Being self sacrificing.

❖ Being Selfless.

Encourage yourself and the people around you to change

- For better.
- Improve their behaviour.
- Enhance their attitude.
- Leave healthier life style
- Try to be stress free.
- Try to improve their behaviour.
- Enhance their attitude.
- Be calm with approach to challenges in live.
- Be tranquil
- Feel comfortable within self.
- Be hassle-free.
- Promote peace.
- Allow nothing to disturb your mind.

Here is some friendly advice for you.

❖ Take a regular inventory of your behaviour and attitude.

❖ Think twice before taking actions.

❖ Be an inventor. Make sure to invest into many good businesses.

❖ Be a pioneer. Be the first person to start something, you can do it. Do not let your dream die, keep the flame of your success going.

❖ Be an originator.

❖ Be creative in ideas.

❖ Break into new grounds.

❖ Be a path founder.

❖ Initiate good things.

❖ Be an enemy to no one.

- ❖ See no evil.
- ❖ Be faithful.
- ❖ Be trustworthy.
- ❖ Advocate for good change.
- ❖ Accommodate the less fortunate.
- ❖ Encourage the broken hearted.
- ❖ Give good advice to the vulnerable.
- ❖ Support the needy.
- ❖ Reward the faithful.

HOW YOU CAN ACCOMPLISH THE HIGHEST LEVEL OF MOTIVATION WITHIN A SHORT TIME.

- Make pledges to yourself.
- Set goals.
- Set targets and pursue them day and night.
- Believe in yourself.
- Get people to help you- Team work.
- Good affirmation daily.
- Dream big dreams, see it in your mind's eye and feel it in your heart.
- Expect and work had for the best.
- Be kind to yourself and to others.
- Take regular breaks, vacations and holiday.
- Make a difference in life.
- Outcome of all the above is big success.

Congratulation!! For you to hold this book in your hands, I believe you want some change in your live. I believe in you, I believe you are a winner and a leader. As a leader you need to motivate yourself and others. You need to possess the qualities of a good leader. What are the qualities of a leader?

The following are the qualities of a leader

- You need to be able to implement effective delegation.
- Be a good coach.
- You should have non intimidating approach.
- Do not create fear in people.
- Be a motivator not a teacher.
- Be a facilitator not an instructor.
- Give positive criticism.
- Let people learn from you.
- Give opportunities.
- Give hope.
- Think of solving problems.
- Give thanks.
- Appreciate people.
- Be generous.
- Be friendly.
- Give constructive feedback.

TO TRULY THINK BEYOND A MILLIONAIRE'S THINKING, THE THINGS TO AVOID ARE AS FOLLOWS:-

- ❖ Do not allow fear to put you away from achieving your goals.
- ❖ Do not back-bite.
- ❖ Do not associate with negative gossips.
- ❖ Avoid swear words.
- ❖ Avoid negative confrontations
- ❖ No fighting.
- ❖ No hatred.
- ❖ No anger.
- ❖ No negative prophecy.
- ❖ No unacceptable attitude.

❖ No abuse.

❖ No victimisation.

❖ No unfriendly gesture.

❖ No un-accommodation posture.

❖ No intimidation.

❖ Avoid annoyance it can only throw people off their balance.

My friend, whatever you find your hands to do, do it diligently, I implore you to be industrious, you need to be meticulous, and I imply you should be assiduous.

In order to make your dream become a reality, you must keep going until you get what you need, most time you might get fifty "no" before you get one "yes", it's alright, keep going, do not give up. Keep going, remember there are people out their who are waiting for your ideas to be discovered, so my advise to you is not to give up but keep going however rough it might look at the moment, my friend keep going. Never see yourself as a failure because you are not, rather you are someone who is just about to discover your destiny so keep going. You are born to win, so do not give up too soon. Keep going because there are lights at the other side of the tunnel. I come to let you know that you should not quit, but keep steady and keep moving on and you will achieve your aims and objectives.

What ever you need just ask for it, be it help, assistance, funds, supports, prayers, whatever it is my friend just ask, and keep asking until you get a yes answer.

CONCLUSION:

Finally, my conclusion will come in a way of encouragement.

I will congratulate you for laying your hands on this book. It is the first step to your success. Well done! But make sure you read it and apply the information to your real life situation, by so doing you will see a big change in your life.

Remember "If it's to be it's up to you" and also remember that "knowledge is just a tool, it is the application of knowledge which is power"

Power is what will make you a millionaire.

Good Luck, go for it. Apply the principles. Start now, do not procrastinate, you can do it, be determined.

God bless you because I'm sure God will crown your effort with success.

Yours truly,

Abimbola Cole (Idris)

ABOUT THE AUTHOR

About Abimbola Cole (Idris)

Her calling is in the area of prosperity, healing and caring. Abi is the writer and author of the best selling book called "How to become a millionaire in a way that is dignifying to God (with all right reserved). She is a motivational speaker, a coach and a teacher of success skills. She is the CEO and founder of "God Transformation Clinic" and "The Lord's Ambassador Organisation".

She is the pastor and prophetess of God's Promises International Christian Centre. Pastor Abimbola Cole is a Philanthropist building houses for the children in need in the developing countries. She is the founder of Africa Philanthropist magazine. Before her calling pastor Abimbola was a midwife with a strong background in medicine. She is also a strong voice in the industry of network marketing. Her passion is to see the body of Christ and every human being delivered from the spirit of poverty, receive wealth transformation and stay prosperous. She has formed a network of prosperous people who are committed to inspire, mentor and instruct other people about how to create freedom, wealth and outrageous success in their lives. She also has a passion for releasing the word of God and seeing the sick receive their healing.

Finally, Abimbola is an editor, a speaker, trainer, coach and consultant on prosperity, healing and wealth transformation.